PRESENTS

How to be more

**confident, sarcastic,
ironic bastard,
in a world
of asshales,
idiots,
and
fools.**

All right reserved.
No part of this book my be reproduced or used
in a manner without written permisson of the copyright owner
except for the use of quotation in a book review.

First paperback edition oktober 2021

© scienta.et.artes

All right reserved.
No part of this book my be reproduced or used
in a manner without written permisson of the copyright owner
except for the use of quotation in a book review.

First paperback edition oktober 2021

© **scienta.et.artes**

Printed in Great Britain
by Amazon